CHRISTMAS

CRACKERS

A Play for children

Willis Hall

Samuel French

and

Heinemann Educational Books

First published 1976

Published jointly by Samuel French Ltd
26 Southampton Street London WC2E 7JE

New York   Toronto   Sydney   Hollywood

and by

Heinemann   Educational   Books   Ltd
48 Charles Street   London   W1X 8AH

and in Edinburgh, Melbourne, Auckland,
Toronto, Singapore, Hong Kong, Kuala
Lumpur, Ibadan, Nairobi, Johannesburg,
Lusaka, New Delhi, Kingston

ISBN (Samuel French) 0 573 05040 6
ISBN (Heinemann) 0 435 23369 6

Made and printed by Latimer Trend & Company Ltd Plymouth

CHARACTERS: Convict Gilbert
Convict Crosby
Detective Constable Grummett
Clara Grummett (his wife)
Alexander Grummett (their son)
Constable Mullins
Constable MacBain
Mavis Dawkins
The Mayor

SETTINGS: A Cheerless Attic
A Police Station
Outside Buckingham Palace
The Empty Stage
A Gloomy Room

ACT ONE
Scene One

*Two escaped convicts, Gilbert and Crosby, are spend-
ing Christmas Eve in a cold, cheerless attic. The room
is bare of furniture, except for a couple of orange boxes.
There are empty baked-bean tins everywhere. Some
slight attempt to capture the festive spirit has been
made: a single balloon hangs from the ceiling and a
solitary Christmas card is pinned on the wall. Gilbert
wears a paper hat, Crosby does not. They are both
eating baked beans straight from the tin. Gilbert forks
a mouthful of beans towards his mouth, and then
stops to sing:*

Gilbert	Away in a manger No jam for his bread The little Lord Jesus Had some dripping instead——
Crosby	Shut up, Gilbert.

*They go back to munching their beans and then, a few
moments later:*

Gilbert	Good King Wenceslas looked out On a poor man in his garden He chucked a bucket of tea-leaves down And said 'I beg your pardon——'
Crosby	I said 'belt up'.
Gilbert	Give us a smile, Crosby. After all, it is Christmas Eve.
Crosby	Christmas Eve? You don't call this Christmas Eve, do you? We were better off in the nick. I don't know why you wanted to escape. Just look at the state of this room. We've got no furniture; I'm freezing to death; we've got no Chrissie tree; we've got no decorations. And all we've got to eat is baked beans.
Gilbert	What's the matter, Croz? Don't you like baked beans?
Crosby	Not for every meal. We've been eating them now for over a month. We'll end up looking like baked beans.
Gilbert	If I hadn't gone out and nicked them, we wouldn't have had anything at all.
Crosby	You're supposed to be a desperate criminal, Gilbert. An international crook of magnitudinous proportions. I sent you out to commit the crime of the century, and what happens? All you come back with is a case of baked beans and a box of Chrissie crackers.
Gilbert	It wasn't my fault. They fell off the back of a lorry. *(He produces a cracker)* Do me a favour, Croz. Pull the last one with me.
Crosby	Certainly not.

Gilbert   Go on, show a bit of the Chrissie spirit.

Crosby   No. I won't.

Gilbert   Why not?

Crosby   Because you always win, that's why not. We've pulled eleven crackers, Gilbert, and you've had every single novelty and paper hat.

Gilbert   I won't win this one. You can win it, Croz. *Come* on.

> *Crosby crosses, dubiously, and takes hold of one end of the cracker. Gilbert stands quite still while Crosby tugs, heaves, strains and puffs. The cracker breaks. Gilbert wins. Crosby falls down*

I'm sorry, Croz. I wasn't trying—honest.

> *No reply, Crosby is sulking*

You can have the paper hat if you want it. I've got one.

> *Still no reply, Crosby continues to sulk. Gilbert takes off the hat he is wearing and replaces it with the new one*

Gilbert   Suit yourself. Hey, Croz, do you want to hear the motto? Listen to this: 'If at first you don't succeed—try, try, try again.'

Crosby   I don't think much of that for a motto. I've tried twelve times to pull a cracker with you, and you've won every one.

Gilbert   It's not my fault, Crosby. Oh, look here! Look at the novelty, Croz. It's a little whistle. Go on, have a look.

> *Crosby, still sulking, turns his back. Gilbert blows the whistle. Crosby is half-won over. Gilbert blows the whistle again. Crosby gives in*

Crosby   Can I have a go?

Gilbert   You can have the whistle, Crozzo—it's a Chrissie prezzie from me to you.

> *Crosby takes the whistle, delighted, and blows it*

And have one of these hats. I don't want two.

> *Crosby accepts a hat and they are friends again*

Crosby   Thanks, Gilly.

Gilbert   Christmas comes but once a year. Peace on earth. Goodwill to-ward men. *(He spots something out of the window)* Hey, Croz! Look up there! A bright star. Isn't that something to be joyous about? Christmas Eve and a bright star in the night sky?

> *Crosby joins Gilbert at the window. They stand gazing up, respectfully, for some moments, then:*

Gilbert   I say, Croz—do you think if we followed that bright star tonight it might lead us to that tiny stable in Jerusalem?

Crosby   I shouldn't think so, Gilly. I should think it would be more

	likely to lead us to Heathrow Airport. It isn't a star isn't that—it's a Jumbo Jet.
Gilbert	Is it?
Crosby	Of course it is. Look at it go. Stars don't pelt across the sky at that speed, Gillo. If they did, you wouldn't be able to follow them—not on a camel.
Gilbert	I wouldn't mind being up in a Jumbo Jet right now, Croz.
Crosby	Up there? What for?
Gilbert	Because I wouldn't mind spending Christmas Eve, two miles high, sitting back in the first-class cabin, noshing a Jumbo Jet Chrissie dinner.
Crosby	You must be raving mad. You wouldn't get me up in one of them things. I'd rather be back in clink. I like both my feet safely on the ground, matey. On terra firma. Inside four walls.
Gilbert	Please yourself. I thought you said, two minutes ago, you didn't fancy spending Christmas inside these four walls?
Crosby	I don't. Not these four walls. And I'll tell you why. Because we haven't got four walls, have we? There's only three. One, two, three. And where we should have a fourth wall, what have we got? We've got all these people staring back at us. *(He glowers at the audience)* What are you all sitting out there for anyway? Haven't you got no homes to go to? Go on. Buzz off!
Gilbert	It's no good shouting at the audience, Crosby. They won't go home until the play's finished.
Crosby	There won't be a play, Gilly, not if I decide to jump into the stalls and duff up one or two silly, stupid grinning faces. I'll make them wish they'd gone to the pictures or a museum. I hate being in Chrissie plays, Gilbert. I do, I really hate it.
Gilbert	Stop moaning, Crosby. You're always moaning.
Crosby	Is it any wonder? With all them stuffed dummies sitting out there, stuffing crisps and sweeties down their throats, watching every move we make? *(To the audience)* How would you like it if we came round to your house and sat and stared at you? It's worse than being in a zoo.
Gilbert	Forget about them, Croz. Let's get out of this room and go and do something really exciting.
Crosby	Such as?
Gilbert	Well, we're supposed to be desperate criminals—why don't we go out and hold up a bank?
Crosby	At this time of night? On Christmas Eve? All the banks will be shut.
Gilbert	How about breaking into a ciggie warehouse?
Crosby	What for? We don't smoke. I've got it! We'll go out and climb through somebody's window and burglarize their house.
Gilbert	Where are we going to find an empty house on a night like this? They'll all be at home watching the telly.

Crosby   No, they won't. Everybody doesn't sit at home and watch the telly.

Gilbert   *Everybody* that I know does.

            With elaborate winks and nudges, Crosby tries to draw Gilbert's attention to the audience

Crosby   Some people go out. To the theatre. There must be dozens and dozens of houses, right at this minute, with nobody in them, just waiting to be burglarized.

Gilbert   I do wish you wouldn't talk in riddles, Crosby.

Crosby   I'll show you what I mean. Hands up all those nice children who want to help their kind Uncle Crosby enjoy a lovely hot Chrissie dinner this year, with turkey and stuffing and Yorkshire pudding.

Gilbert   Yorkshire pudding?

Crosby   What's wrong with that?

Gilbert   You don't eat Yorkshire pudding with turkey, Croz.

Crosby   Don't you?

Gilbert   Not to the best of my knowledge.

Crosby   I'll start again. Hands up all those children who want to help their Uncle Crosby get his hands on a scrumptious Chrissie dinner with turkey and stuffing and mint sauce?

Gilbert   That's better.

Crosby   Come on, kids, stick your hands up. 'Cos I'm going to tell you what I want you to do. Tell your mummy or your daddy—or your teacher—whoever you came with—that you want to go to the lavvy. Then meet me in the foyer and give me your addresses. Then, while Uncle Gilbert keeps you entertained with some riddles and some paper-tearing, I'll nip out and burglarize your houses and nick some mince-pies and Chrissie pud.

Gilbert   We can't do that, Croz!

Crosby   Why not? Don't you know any riddles?

Gilbert   You can't go out and burglarize the houses of the members of the audience.

Crosby   We can if we want.

Gilbert   At Christmas time? Do me a favour. Show *some* respect. Besides, Equity would never stand for it.

Crosby   Go on, Gilly. Let me burglarize a house—just one.

Gilbert   No.

Crosby   Go on. What about a mansion. If anybody lives in a mansion, they're not going to miss a couple of mince-pies and a bit of Chrissie pud. Hands up all those kids who live in mansions?

Gilbert   No!

Crosby   Give me one good reason why not.

Gilbert   Because it's wrong, Crosby. It's anti-social. A typical example of man's inhumanity to man. Besides, whichever kids' houses

	we burglarize, their dads might find out it was us and duff us up.
Crosby	I'll soon solve that. Listen, kids, we want to find out who's got the littlest dad in the audience. All those kids with big, tough dads, keep your hands down—but all those with scrawny, weedy, titchy dads who couldn't knock the skin off a school dinner rice pudding, stick your hands up. Come on, kids. You can't all have massive dads.
Gilbert	No, Crosby. We're not going to do it.
Crosby	Who's going to stop us?
Voice	*(from the audience)* I'm going to stop you, Gilbert and Crosby. I intend to put an end to these goings-on.
Crosby	Who said that, Gilly?
Gilbert	Search me, Crozzo.

A seedy figure in a grubby suit, macintosh, large boots and bowler hat, has made its way to the front of the stage from out of the audience. He is Detective Constable Stephen Grummett.

Grummett	I said it. There'll be no burglarizing of houses of members of the audience—not so long as I am in the theatre.
Gilbert	Who are you?
Grummett	A member of the audience.

Grummett makes his way on to the stage.

Gilbert	Go back. We can't have members of the audience coming on the stage while we're in the middle of a play. Anyway, he was only joking, weren't you, Croz?
Crosby	'Course I was.
Gilbert	He wouldn't burglarize the audience—would you, Croz?
Crosby	Never in a million years. I wouldn't dream of it.
Gilbert	He was only saying that because it's in the play.
Crosby	I've been rehearsing it for weeks.
Grummett	We'll see about that. *(He produces a gun)* Hands up!

Gilbert and Crosby raise their hands in the air.

As well as being a member of the audience, I am also proud to belong to the finest police force in the world. The British Constabulary! My name is Detective Constable Grummett, C.I.D. In fact, now that I come to think of it, I seem to recall that I've had the somewhat dubious pleasure of arresting you two criminals before, in a previous Christmas entertainment. Last Christmas, same stage, different play but same two desperate criminals.

Crosby	Oh, crikey, Gilly, it's him!
Gilbert	We weren't doing anything this time, were we?

Grummett   Keep your hands up high! Weren't doing anything? That's a laugh, if you'll pardon the expression. What about threatening to burglarize the members of the audience? What about corrupting little children? And what about appearing in a play that contravenes the Trades Descriptions Act?

Crosby   How do you mean, Detective Constable Grummett?

Grummett   What I say. I came here for a bit of a rest. My missis has dragged me round the shops all morning. I paid for seats to see a Chrissie play. It's my birthday as well—this was going to be my birthday treat to me. I sent the missis out to the foyer for some iced lollies. I sat back, hoping to enjoy myself—expecting to see 'Jack and the Beanstalk' or 'Cinderella' or one of those. Instead of which, I'm confronted with two desperate criminals, minnying round the stage and planning to nick Chrissie pud from members of the audience.

Gilbert   It's still a Chrissie play, Detective Constable Grummett.

Grummett   With scenery like this? A proper thieves' kitchen if ever I saw one!

            Gilbert and Crosby back away as if to make a run for it

Grummett   Don't move! Keep those hands up! I've got my little lad sitting in those stalls as well. What do you think a show like this is going to do to an innocent mind like his? You ought to be 'X' certificated. Christmas play my foot!

Crosby   It is, Detective Constable Grummett. We had a Chrissie star in it earlier on.

Grummett   That was a Jumbo Jet, you big fibber. I was sitting out there watching.

Crosby   There's a real Chrissie star in it later, Detective Constable Grummett, just you wait and see.

Gilbert   I'll tell you something else we've got you don't usually see in Chrissie plays.

Grummett   What's that?

Gilbert   A spooky, green, grinning skelegog—do you want to see it? *(Calling offstage)* Can we have the spooky, green, grinning skelegog on, please?

            A spooky, green, grinning skeleton descends from above and dangles in front of Detective Constable Grummett. Grummett staggers back in fear and trembling.

Grummett   Ow! Oooh! Help! Mother! Take it away, I don't like it!

Gilbert   Come on, Crozzo, run for it!

            Gilbert and Crosby take to their heels and seek refuge in the audience. The skeleton disappears from whence it came. Grummett pulls himself together and blows several blasts on his whistle.

Grummett   Seize them! Stop them! Grab those hardened criminals! *(Calling into the wings)* If there are any reputable actors out there who can portray the roles of fearless British bobbies—will they come forward, please!

> *Grummett gives a couple more toots on his whistle. Two constables, Mullins and Macbain run on to the stage.*

Grummett   After them, lads! Don't let them get away!

> *Macbain and Mullins pursue Gilbert and Crosby through the auditorium. When they have gone, Grummet addresses the audience.*

Right then! Pay attention and sit up straight. If you awkward kids want to help hardened villains escape, you be like that. But don't think you're going to get away with it scot-free. You ought to be ashamed of yourselves, parents and children alike, coming to see a play about a couple of rascals, when you could have been sat in the stalls of a respectable theatre, shouting out 'I believe in fairies!' And helping poor little Tinkerbell to live. Either that, or else cheering on Ratty and Mole in their annual epic struggle against the stoats and weasels. Before I've finished, I'm going to turn this load of disgusting rubbish into a proper pantomime. With a fairy for a start. You all love fairies, don't you? *(Cries of 'No')* You little horrors! You get worse and worse! *(Calling offstage)* Who's in charge out there? I want all this criminal scenery off the stage, and some proper panto scenery in its place! Come on! Shift it! I am an officer from New Scotland Yard and my word is law!

> *Grummett strides off. The lights fade. A pause, then Gilbert and Crosby enter from the rear of the auditorium and make their way through the stalls.*

Gilbert   Come on, Croz—I think we've given them the slip at last.

Crosby   I hope so, Gilly. I wouldn't like to meet Detective Constable Grummett again, not this year anyway.

Gilbert   Hey, Crosby! *Look!*

Crosby   Where?

Gilbert   Up there! There *is* a Chrissie star!

Crosby   I can't see one. *Where?*

Gilbert   There! A bright star hanging low in the night sky, Crozzo!

Crosby   I can't see one. I bet it's that Jumbo Jet again.

Gilbert   It isn't, Croz. It isn't moving. It *is* a star. Look up there!

Crosby   Hey, Gilly, you're right!

> *With Gilbert and Crosby, we can now see a pinpoint of light on the dark stage.*

Crosby   If it's hanging over a stable, Gilbert, bags I first pat of the oxen.

They have arrived at the front of the stalls and they tiptoe, tentatively, on to the stage.

Scene Two

The 'starlight' grows stronger, and proves to be the light above a police station. There is a desk, a large notice-board, and a door marked 'CELL'.

Gilbert and Crosby show consternation at finding themselves inside a police station.

Crosby   You silly, stupid nana, Gilbert! You've done it again. It's not a star at all! It's a cop-shop light.

Gilbert   You're right, Crozzo. It is.

Crosby   I hate police stations. I do, Gillo, I really hate them. Let's get out of here, smartish.

Gilbert   Come on, Crozzo—quick, there's somebody coming.

Gilbert and Crosby nip off on one side as Mullins and MacBain enter from the other, very much out of breath.

Mullins   That's really tired me out, chasing those two villains, Mr MacBain.

MacBain   And me. I'm positively out of puff.

Mullins   Do you think we've seen the end of them?

MacBain   Most definitely, Mr Mullins. I'll tell you what—we'd better have! I can think of nicer ways of spending Christmas than chasing two hardened criminals round the auditorium.

Mullins   Me too. Just let them show their noses anywhere near here again, and they'll find themselves behind bars. We seem to have a customer.

Clara Grummett enters, accompanied by her son, Alexander. Clara is carrying a bulging shopping-bag over one arm, and holding aloft an ice-lolly in each hand. Alexander also has an ice-lolly.

MacBain   'Ello, 'ello, 'ello?

Mullins   'Evening, all.

MacBain   What's all this 'ere?

Clara   I'm looking for my husband. He hasn't been here, has he, by any chance?

MacBain   That depends, ma'am. Could you give us his name and description?

Clara	He's called Detective Constable Grummett. He wears big boots and a bowler hat.
Mullins	Is he appearing in this play?
Clara	No, but he's supposed to be watching it. We all are. This is our son, Alexander.
Mullins	How do, young man?

Alexander sticks his tongue out at Mullins.

Watch it!

Clara	That's naughty, Alexander! Mumsie's very cross. *(Back to Mullins)* We were in the stalls and he sent us out to get some ice-lollies. When we came back with them, he'd disappeared. I've got to find him soon—they're starting to melt.

At some point during the above Mullins has taken off his hat and put it on the desk. Now, as Alexander leans over the desk, the top of his ice-lolly drops off the stick and into Mullins's hat.

Mullins	Do you mind, young feller-me-lad? The top of your lolly has just dropped into my policeman's hat. Would you mind picking it out?
Alexander	Pick it out yourself.
Mullins	I beg your pardon!
Alexander	You heard. My dad's a real detective, not just an actor dressed up as a crumby old constable. Mum, can I have an orange squash next?
Clara	No, you cannot, Alexander. Not if you speak like that to members of the cast. Besides, Mummy's busy. She's trying to discover where Daddy is.
MacBain	I'm afraid you won't find him up here, ma'am. This is the stage. That's the audience out there.
Mullins	Just a minute, Mr MacBain. There was a chap up here not long ago. He had a bowler hat on *and* big boots.
MacBain	You're right, Mr Mullins, so there was! He was blowing a policeman's whistle, too. It was him that sent us off chasing that pair of villains.
Clara	That sounds like him. Nosey-parkering. He's always interfering where he isn't wanted. He went up on the stage at Butlin's once and showed me up. It was in a talent contest.
MacBain	Did he win it?
Clara	Did he heck. He tried to sing 'If I Ruled The World'—he didn't even know the words. I'll show him who rules the world when I lay my hands on him. These lollies are starting to dribble down my arms. Come along, Alexy-walexy, Mummy's in a hurry.
Alexander	No.

Clara	Alexander Grummett! I hope I didn't hear you say 'no' to Mummy?
Alexander	I'm thirsty.
Clara	Oh—very well. Come along. We'll see if there's a nice kind stage-manager who keeps orange squash hidden away for good little boysies.

> *Alexander and Clara have left the police station and are moving off-stage as MacBain calls after them:*

MacBain	Come back, ma'am. You can't go through there, it's not allowed!

> *But Clara and Alexander have already gone. Mullins is puzzled.*

Mullins	I don't remember seeing them at rehearsals.
MacBain	Of course you don't—she isn't in it. She's a member of the audience.
Mullins	I'm not at all happy with the way this performance is going.
MacBain	Look out. Look busy. Pretend to be acting. Somebody's coming.

> *Detective Constable Grummett enters and pauses to address the audience.*

Grummett	Sit up straight! No talking! I've just spent the last five minutes going round in circles. Nobody in the theatre knows anything about anybody. I shall have to take steps regarding having the Arts Council grant reduced here. And I haven't finished with you lot neither.

> *Grummett moves into the police station.*

Are you the two brave lads who went off in pursuit of Gilbert and Crosby, the hardened criminals?

> *Mullins and MacBain nod their heads.*

Mullins	I'm Constable Mullins.
MacBain	I'm Constable MacBain.
Grummett	And did you nobble them for me? Did you manage to feel their collars?

> *Mullins and MacBain shake their heads.*

MacBain	Are you, by any chance, Detective Constable Grummett?
Grummett	Who told you my name?
MacBain	Your wife. Mrs Grummett.

> *Grummett glances around, anxiously.*

Grummett	Is she about?
MacBain	She was. She's gone off looking for you.

> *Grummett is relieved.*

Mullins	Your ice-lolly's melting.

Grummett   I've bigger things on my plate than ice-lollies at this immediate
           moment. I shan't rest until those arch-fiends, Gilbert and Crosby,
           are safely behind bars. I've called in here to request the further
           assistance of you two constables to apprehend the villains.
           They're wanted men.

MacBain   What are they wanted for?

Grummett   All kinds of things. They escaped from a Christmas play last
           year.

MacBain   I don't think we can spare the time.

Mullins   We're in a play ourselves.

Grummett   Plays? Plays? Never mind about plays. I'm talking about real
           life. Anyway, this play you're in is a right load of old cods-
           wallop.

MacBain   What's wrong with it?

Mullins   We've been in worse.

Grummett   It isn't fit for kiddies, for one thing—and it isn't seasonal for
           another. I'm having it all changed. I'm taking it over and turn-
           ing it into a pantomime with a Chrissie fairy. I shall have every
           member of the cast, including you, suitably and seasonally
           attired. I'm even thinking of having a panto horse!

MacBain   Oh, great!

Mullins   Smashing! Can we be it?

MacBain   Bags I the front end!

Mullins   We've been a panto horse before.

           *MacBain and Mullins adopt the position of a panto-
           mime horse and gallop around the stage. Then, facing
           front:*

MacBain   Ask me what four and four is?

Grummett   What's four and four?

           MacBain stamps his hoof on the ground nine times

Grummett   That was nine.

MacBain   No, it wasn't.

Grummett   Yes, it was. Anyway, pack it in. I didn't say I *was* having a
           panto horse, just that I was *thinking* about having one, that's
           all. But you scratch my back, I'll scratch yours. Real life comes
           first—it's more important than play-acting. You two help me to
           capture Gilbert and Crosby, and I'll see you're all right. Suppos-
           ing I was to tell you this could lead to better acting parts?

MacBain   What sort of better acting parts?

Grummett   Supposing I was to tell you that the New Scotland Yard
           Dramatic Society was looking for a pair of bright sparks to play
           two Chief Inspectors in a murder thriller?

MacBain   Chief Inspectors?

Mullins   When?

MacBain   Where?

Grummett   They're putting it on in an open-air theatre in a public car-park for the Traffic Wardens' New Year Party.

Mullins   What do you want us to do?

Grummett   It's my belief that Gilbert and Crosby are still lurking about somewhere in the theatre. I'll have a scout around backstage while you two search the audience. They could be masquerading as a pair of paying customers and sitting it out, as bold as brass, in a couple of seats in the stalls. If you lay hold of them, blow your whistles, slip your handcuffs on 'em, and I'll be here in two seconds flat.

He crosses downstage and addresses the audience.

And you rotten lot can just sit up straight and give them your full co-operation for a change. Now, is that clear? I wouldn't be at all surprised if one or two of you ruffians turned out to be in cahoots with Gilbert and Crosby—and if my suspicions are confirmed, you will be sorry!

With which, Grummett stalks off. Mullins and MacBain look at each other, doubtfully.

MacBain   What do you think, Mr Mullins?

Mullins   What about?

MacBain   What he said. Now that he's gone, shall we get on with the play, or should we go and search the audience for those desperate criminals?

Mullins   I suppose, by rights, we should get on with the play.

MacBain   We should really.

Mullins   On the other hand, I wouldn't half like to have a crack at acting the part of a Chief Inspector.

MacBain   So would I. It would be a step up from playing constables all the time.

Mullins   I vote we go and look for the criminals in the audience.

Mullins and MacBain approach the audience rather nervously, but start off in true 'constable-acting' style.

MacBain   'Ello, 'ello, 'ello?

Mullins   'Evening, all.

MacBain   What's all this 'ere? Right then, kids—dads, mums, teachers, and other supernumaries—it is believed that two dangerous criminals, Gilbert and Crosby, may be sitting out there posing as members of the audience.

Mullins   It's quite all right. There's no need to panic.

MacBain   No cause for alarm. Mr Mullins and myself have been acting policemen's parts long enough to be more than capable of dealing with a couple of hard-case layabouts.

Mullins	Could we have the lights up, please?
	Bring up house lights.
MacBain	Thank you. And now, my colleague, Mr Mullins, will step forward and quickly run his eyes along the stalls. If Gilbert and Crosby are out there anywhere, he'll nail them right away—he has their exact descriptions imprinted on his mind.
Mullins	No, I haven't.
MacBain	Haven't you?
Mullins	No. I don't know what they look like. You do it.
MacBain	I don't know what they look like, either.
Mullins	You chased them through the stalls.
MacBain	So did you.
Mullins	I chased them, yes. But I only saw them from behind.
MacBain	So did I. Do you think if you saw them from behind again you could recognize them?
Mullins	Do you?
MacBain	I might.
Mullins	I might, too. But you can't hold an identity parade with everybody back-to-front . . . Can you?
MacBain	*(to the audience)* Would you all stand up, please? Come on, everybody—on your feet. Come on. Any person who remains seated during this identity parade will be taken as having something to hide, and will be considered a Number One Suspect. Everybody up. Now, turn round with your backs to us.
	The audience turns round and faces the back of the auditorium.
	What do you think, Mr Mullins?
Mullins	I don't know what to think. I've seen some funny sights in the theatre, but I've never seen the back of an audience before. It's enough to put you off.
MacBain	Turn round again.
	The audience turns round and faces the front again
	Sit down. Lights out.
	The house lights go down.
Mullins	It's no good, Mr MacBain. Even if they are out there, we'll never recognize them.
MacBain	If only we had their photographs. Just a minute! We could make Identikit pictures of them!
Mullins	Of course we could! *(Then, suddenly puzzled)* How could we do that?
	MacBain produces a large box which is labelled: 'IDENTIKIT'.

MacBain	Easy. With our official New Scotland Yard Bumper Identikit Outfit.
Mullins	Dead simple. Why didn't I think of that? *(Again puzzled)* What is it, Mr MacBain?
MacBain	You *know* what it is, Mr Mullins. You've had it all explained. We have these blank faces and we stick on eyes and mouths and noses and so forth to look like Gilbert and Crosby.
Mullins	Fantastic! Great! What do we do that for?
MacBain	So that we'll know what they look like when we see them. Give me a hand.

> *MacBain and Mullins set up the Identikit outfit—either on the police station notice-board or on an easel, downstage. The Identikit may best be constructed from a large metal sheet, covered with white paper, on which can be stuck eyes, noses, etc., by the aid of small magnets.*

Mullins	What do we do next?
MacBain	Now we put the faces on the board and make them look like Gilbert and Crosby
Mullins	I'm really looking forward to this bit. Let's get on with it.
MacBain	We've hit a snag.
Mullins	Already?
MacBain	We can't do Identikit pictures of Gilbert and Crosby because we don't know what they look like, do we?
Mullins	Only from behind. I knew there'd be a catch to it. Let's take it down again.
MacBain	I've had another idea!
Mullins	Is it better than the last one?
MacBain	*They* know what Gilbert and Crosby look like.
Mullins	Who do?
MacBain	*(secretively indicating the audience)* They do. *Them.*
Mullins	The audience?
MacBain	Certainly. They can help us make up the Identikit pictures.
Mullins	Do you think they will?
MacBain	I'll ask them. *(To the audience)* How about it, kids? Will you help Constable Mullins and me do the Identikit pictures of Gilbert and Crosby? *(Audience: 'Yes!')* Because you know what they look like and we've never seen them. This is what we'll do. I'll ask the questions, you tell me the answers, and Constable Mullins can stick the Identikit pictures on the board.
Mullins	Can I really? I'm going to enjoy this.
MacBain	First of all—and this is very important, so think carefully before you answer, kids—faces. Did Gilbert and Crosby both have faces? *(Audience: 'Yes!')* Are you sure? *(Audience: 'Yes!')* They seem unanimous on that one. Two faces, Mr Mullins.

> *Mullins draws two large circles on the Identikit board.*

Mullins   Two faces.

MacBain   Jolly good, Mr Mullins. Well done. We're coming on a treat. *(Back to the audience)* What about eyes? Had they both got eyes? How many? Two? Two eyes, Mr Mullins, if you would be so kind?

Mullins   Two little eyes.

> *Mullins puts a magnetic eye in the centre of each blank face.*

MacBain   How's that? Is it beginning to look like them? *(Cries of 'No!' from the audience)* What's wrong with it? Oh! *Four* eyes? Well, somebody over there distinctly told me two. Four eyes, if you please, Mr Mullins.

> *Mullins adds two more eyes, possibly putting them all on one face, and MacBain ad-libbing against the audience's displeasure. The process continues, Mullins adding features to the Identikit board, until both faces contain eyes, ears, nose and mouth.*

(To the audience) How's that, then? Is that them, would you say? Have we succeeded in capturing their individual likenesses? What's your opinion, Mr Mullins?

Mullins   Speaking personally, I'm highly satisfied.

MacBain   *(doubtful)* Really? You don't say? I can't help feeling something's missing—somehow.

Mullins   Such as what?

MacBain   I don't know. I can't quite put my finger on it, but looking at what you've got there—I mean, be fair, Mr Mullins, them two faces could belong to anybody.

> *Mullins and MacBain study the faces intently, before:*

(Back to the audience) Anything else? Did they have any distinguishing marks or features you can bring to mind? I know! Were they wearing anything on their heads? *(Audience: 'Yes!')* We're getting warm now, Mr Mullins—they said, 'Yes'.

Mullins   Keep at it, Mr MacBain!

MacBain   Now, think carefully, kids. What were they wearing on their heads. What? I can't hear if you all shout at once. Gloves? Football boots? *Hats!* Did you hear that, Mr Mullins? They had hats on. Have a scout round in the Identikit box and see if you can find a couple of hats in there.

> *Mullins puts a couple of cut-out bowler hats on top of the heads.*

Mullins   How's them suit?

MacBain   *(to the audience)* Hats like that? *(Audience: 'No!')* Try again, Mr Mullins.

        Mullins tries again, this time with chefs' hats. Again the audience, prompted by MacBain, cries 'No!' And next, Mullins tries out a couple of policemen's hats, identical to the ones that he and MacBain are wearing.

        (To the audience) How about that kind? *(Audience: 'No!' MacBain glances at the Identikit board)* Hang on a tiny second, Mr Mullins. I've seen hats like that somewhere before.

        Mullins also examines the board closely.

Mullins   Now that you come to mention it, they do look a bit familiar.

        MacBain and Mullins study the Identikit faces, then turn and study each other's face, and then back again to peer at the Identikit board. Something stirs at the back of their minds.

MacBain   That face reminds me of somebody, if only I could put a name to it.

        Mullins is staring at the other face on the Identikit board

Mullins   And that one rings a bell with me—I've got his name on the tip of my tongue.

        They glance at each other again, and the penny drops.

MacBain
& Mullins } It's you! You're him!

        They grapple with each other. During the struggle, they both manage to get their whistles out and, simultaneously, blow several short, sharp blasts. Grummett races in from the back of the auditorium.

Grummett   Hang on to them, lads! Don't let them escape!

MacBain   I've got one, Detective Constable Grummett!

Mullins   Me too! Mine won't get away!

        By the time Grummett arrives on stage, MacBain and Mullins have both succeeded in handcuffing each other, so that all four of their wrists are manacled. They have also realized their mistake and are suitably sheepish.

Grummett   You pair of blithering idiots! What's your game?

Mullins   We meant well, Detective Constable Grummett. We got carried away.

MacBain   We did our best. It was a case of over-enthusiasm, that's all.

Grummett   It was a case of over-acting, if you ask me. You were playing it for laughs again. Demeaning the role of the British bobby on

	the English stage. Actors! You're all the same. Get those silly handcuffs off immediately.
MacBain	I can't undo mine. I lost the key at the dress-rehearsal.
Mullins	I never had a key to mine—I've always had to borrow his.
Grummett	Get back to your dressing-rooms, this instant! And pray that the stage-management can help you out of those handcuffs, 'cos I know I can't!

> *Mullins and MacBain go off, still handcuffed together, embarrassed and ashamed. Grummett addresses the audience.*

As for you young hooligans, you think because it's Christmas you can get away with anything—you'll find you can't. I've just been having a word with the theatre manager. He agrees with me. It's not family entertainment what's happening up here. He's given me *carte blanche*—I can put on whatever pantomime I like. *(Calling into the wings)* Do you hear me? I want all this scenery taken down to be used in evidence. Come on! Chop, chop! Shift it then! I want it swopped for an enchanted castle or a magical fairyland palace or something of that ilk. Do you think you can manage it without making a botch of things for once?

> *The police station set begins to move.*

Not like that, you stupid stage-hands! You're spoiling the theatrical illusion. Put the lights out first. *(The house lights go down)* That's a bit more like it!

> *Grummett goes off. The stage is in total darkness. Gilbert and Crosby enter from the rear of the auditorium.*

Gilbert	It's all right, Croz. They've gone. The coast is clear.
Crosby	Where are we going now, Gilly?
Gilbert	Down there, of course. Back on the stage.
Crosby	Do we have to? Do you think it's safe?
Gilbert	'Course it is. Come on, Croz. Let's get on with the play. Hey, Crozzo! Look! There's that Chrissie star again!

> *The pin-point of light has appeared again, glowing in the darkness of the centre-stage.*

Crosby	That settles it, Gilbert. I'm not going on there.
Gilbert	Why not?
Crosby	Isn't it obvious? It's going to be that cop-shop again.
Gilbert	No, it isn't, Croz. They turn the lights down to change the scenery. They never come up on the same scene twice. It will be the Chrissie star this time. You wait and see.

> *They move on to the stage.*

Scene Three

As Gilbert and Crosby move on to the stage, the lights come up on a wall with a sentry-box at each end. In the centre of the wall is a royal coat-of-arms. The wall also contains some graffiti: 'E.R. luvs H.R.H.' 'Q.E.2 rules O.K.?' The 'star' disappears.

Crosby   Where are we, Gilly? I've never seen this scenery before.

Gilbert   Look out! There's somebody coming!

They turn to flee in the opposite direction, but:

Crosby   There's another somebody coming from there as well.

Gilbert   Hide, Croz!

Gilbert ducks into one of the sentry-boxes. Crosby attempts to squeeze in with him, but there is not enough room for two. After some kerfuffle, they take up hiding-places in separate sentry-boxes. Just in time. Two Sentries march on from opposite sides of the stage. They wear busbies; long guardsmen's overcoats; and carry rifles on their shoulders. They march across the stage, impressively, passing each other, and going off again. Grummett returns, entering from behind the wall to examine his handiwork.

Grummett   That's better! That's more like a bit of panto scenery. *(But he double-takes as he realizes what the wall represents)* No, it isn't! This is worse than before! *(Calling into the wings)* I said a *fairyland* palace, you idiots! This is *Buckingham Palace*! We can't perform a pantomime outside the house of our Sovereign Queen! If we take the mickey out of her, I'll never get my M.B.E. Who put this palace scenery on? Come on, come clean! He'll get fifteen years before I'm through with him. All right, if you won't own up, I'll come out there and commence enquiries. *(To the audience)* You little monsters can sit tight—nobody's allowed to act in front of this scenery until I return!

Grummett strides off. Gilbert and Crosby come out of their hiding-places.

Crosby   I hate Detective Constable Grummett. I do, I really hate him, Gilbert.

Gilbert   He's gone now.

Crosby   And I'm not particularly fond of you. I don't know how you manage to do it—every time. First you land us bang inside a cop-shop, and this time you've got us outside Buckingham Palace.

Gilbert	It wasn't my fault, Crosby. We were following that Chrissie star.
Crosby	You and your star! That wasn't a star, Gilbert. If it was a star, where is it now?
Gilbert	I can't see it now. It must have gone behind a cloud.
Crosby	Star! That was a light in a bedroom window. It could have been Her Majesty the Queen, Gilly, hanging up her stocking and calling it a day.
Gilbert	Here, Croz, I wonder what she had for supper?
Crosby	Dunno. But I'll tell you what she didn't have, Gillo—baked flippin' beans!
Gilbert	Come on, Croz.
Crosby	Where to now?
Gilbert	To find a ladder, of course.
Crosby	What do we want a ladder for?
Gilbert	To nip over that wall. We're going to find that star.
Crosby	Have you gone raving bonkers, Gilbert? We can't go over that wall. That's Buckingham Palace. That'd be treason. We'd end up in the Tower of London if we nipped over there.
Gilbert	It's only scenery, Crosby.
Crosby	I'm not so sure. Since Detective Constable Grummett showed up, I'm not sure any longer what's scenery and what's real.
Gilbert	It's scenery, Croz. You look at it close.
Crosby	Well them two guardsmen definitely weren't scenery. And neither were those rifles they were carrying. And I know for a certain fact that Detective Constable Grummett's real. Supposing they catch us climbing over the wall?
Gilbert	They won't, Croz.
Crosby	How do you know they won't?
Gilbert	I've had a great idea.
Crosby	Oh, no! Not another. I hate your great ideas, Gilly. I do, I really hate them.
Gilbert	You'll like this one. We're going to create a diversion.
Crosby	Are we really? Fantastic! What's a diversion, Gilbert?
Gilbert	I'll tell you later. Let's go and find that ladder.

> *They go off. The two sentries return, from opposite sides of the stage again, perform some intricate drill movements and then take up their posts in front of the sentry-boxes. They stand smartly to attention for some moments, before one of them bends his knees in a very unguardsman-like manner, and we realize that they are:*

MacBain	'Ello, 'ello, 'ello?
Mullins	'Evening, all!

MacBain   What's all this 'ere?

        They recognize each other.

        It's Mr Mullins, isn't it?

Mullins   Aren't you Mr MacBain?

MacBain   Well I'm blowed! I didn't recognize you dressed up like that.

Mullins   Nor me you. Somebody stuck me in this, uniform, muttered something about 'the show having to go on , and pushed me on the stage.

MacBain   Same here. I've only played policeman parts before. Apart from once being a panto horse.

Mullins   Same here.

MacBain   'Ello, 'ello, 'ello?

Mullins   'Evening all!

MacBain   What's all this 'ere?

Mullins   What are we going to do if anyone shows up?

MacBain   How do you mean?

Mullins   I mean, what words can we say? We've only learned policemen's words.

MacBain   We'll have to wing it. We'll improvize. We're actors, aren't we? We'll make words up as we go along.

Mullins   Do you think that's going to work?

MacBain   I hope so. Look out! There's somebody coming now.

        Detective Constable Grummett returns, pushing a prop basket. He pauses to study the two sentries, suspiciously. MacBain and Mullins exchange nervous glances, then:

        'Ello, 'ello, 'ello?

Mullins   'Evening, all!

MacBain   What's all this 'ere? I must ask you to accompany me as far as the station for questioning. *(He pauses, grins foolishly at Grummett, and:)* That wasn't very good, was it?

Grummett   You're those two coppers, aren't you? What's supposed to be working for me?

Mullins   We don't know what we're doing in these sentries' uniforms— somebody stuck us in 'em and pushed us on.

Grummett   That's partly down to me. I've taken over full control of this entertainment, but somebody got the scenery wrong. I've got some proper panto costumes in this basket, I'll be issuing them to everybody, forthwith. Carry on for now as sentries while I get things sorted out.

        Grummett moves to leave.

MacBain   You wouldn't do us a favour, would you, before you go?

Grummett   Such as?

MacBain	Give us some sentries' words to say. In case anybody else shows up.
Mullins	We only know policemen's words.

And they go into their routine again, complete with knee-bends.

MacBain	'Ello, 'ello, 'ello?
Mullins	'Evening, all!
MacBain	What's all this——
Grummett	Orlright, orlright, we've done all that. If anyone walks on this stage you stick your gun out at them and you say: Halt, who goes there? Friend or foe?
MacBain	That's good! *(Practising)* Halt, who goes there? Friend or foe? I like that. Ta.
Grummett	And you say: Advance, friend, and be reckernized.
Mullins	Great! Advance, friend, and be reckernized. Terrific!
Grummett	And keep an eye on the basket for me.

Grummett goes off. MacBain and Mullins pull themselves up proudly, with new confidence.

MacBain	Do you fancy having a little rehearsal?
Mullins	I wouldn't mind.
MacBain	Halt, who friends there? Goes or foes? That's not right, is it?

Mullins shakes his head

I'll start again. From the top. Halt, who foes goes? Friends or theres? 'Ello, 'ello, 'ello?

Mullins	'Evening, all—— Now you're getting me at it.
MacBain	I never was a quick learner.
Mullins	Same here. I like to have my words written down so I can learn them on the bus. We'll never get them right.
MacBain	Yes, we will. *(He indicates the audience)* If they give us a hand. Will you help us with our words, kids? *(Audience: 'Yes!')*
Mullins	How can they help us?
MacBain	They can say them for us.
Mullins	Is that allowed?
MacBain	*(shrugs)* I don't suppose we'd get away with it at the National Theatre or the Royal Shakespeare Company, but they're not so fussy here. *(To the audience)* Whenever I stick my gun out, like this, will you all shout—— *(To Mullins)* What is it, again?
Mullins	Halt, who goes there? Friend or foe? *(To the audience)* And whenever I stick my gun out, can you shout—— *(To MacBain)* What was my one?
MacBain	Advance, friend, and be reckernized.
Mullins	That's it. Can you manage that, kids?
MacBain	We'll have a rehearsal, shall we? Ready?

MacBain brings his rifle to the on-guard position. The audience yell: 'Halt, who goes there? Friend or foe?' Mullins brings his rifle to the on-guard position. The audience yell: 'Advance, friend, and be reckernized.'

Smashing, kids!

Mullins	Couldn't be better. I've got no worries at all now, about being a sentry.
Mullins	Nor me.
MacBain	It's a load off my shoulders, having somebody to say the lines. It means I can concentrate on the drill movements. Fancy a march right round the outside of the theatre?
Mullins	Why not? And the last one back is a silly sausage.
MacBain	By the right—quick march! Lef', ri', lef', ri', lef'-ri'-lef'!

Mullins and MacBain march off and, immediately, Gilbert and Crosby tip-toe on.

Gilbert	Did you hear that, Croz?
Crosby	They're not sentries at all. It's them two coppers.
Gilbert	Yes, but did you hear them ask the audience to say their sentries' words for them?
Crosby	Halt, who goes there? Friend or foe? Advance, friend, and be reckernized. They're not difficult words to learn at all.
Gilbert	Bit of a cheek, if you ask me. You'd think they'd take the trouble to sit in a corner and learn them. Here, Croz, I've had an idea.
Crosby	Not another one, Gilly?
Gilbert	You will like this one. What do you say if we play a trick on Detective Constable Grummett? We'll get the kids to change the words.
Crosby	I do like that idea, Gilbert.
Gilbert	How about it, kids? Would you like to trick Detective Constable Grummett? *(Audience: 'Yes!')*
Crosby	What are you going to get them to say?
Gilbert	Listen, kids. When Grummett comes back to see his sentries, this is what I want you to do. When the first sentry sticks his gun out, you shout out what he said: 'Halt, who goes there? Friend or foe?' But when Grummett shouts back 'friend', you all shout out: 'Advance, fishface, and be fossilized!'
Crosby	That's great, Gilbert. I really do like that. Advance, fishface, and be fossilized!
Gilbert	Can you do that, kids? *(Audience: 'Yes!')* We'll have a rehearsal, shall we? I'll be both the sentries and Crosby can be Detective Constable Grummett. Don't forget, the first time I stick a gun out, you shout: Halt, who goes there? Friend or

foe? And then when he shouts friend, you shout back:
Advance, fishface, and be fossilized! Ready?

Crosby   I'm being Grummett and I'm coming now.

> *Crosby struts forward, aping Grummett. Gilbert pokes
> out an imaginary rifle. Audience: 'Halt, who goes there?
> Friend or Foe?'*

Friend!

> *Audience: 'Advance, fishface, and be fossilized!'*

That'll be really terrific. He'll go spare, will Grummett, when he
gets called fishface. He will, he'll go stark, raving bonkers.

Gilbert   Especially when he gets called fishface on his birthday.

Crosby   Is it his birthday?

Gilbert   Don't you remember? He said he came here for his birthday
treat. That's what my diversion's going to be.

Crosby   What? Detective Constable Grummett's birthday? I don't call
that a diversion, Gilbert.

Gilbert   We're going to get the audience to sing 'Happy Birthday' to
him.

Crosby   We can't do that!

Gilbert   Why not?

Crosby   Because I hate him, that's why not. I do. I really hate him. I'm not
singing 'Happy Birthday' to him.

Gilbert   Not the *proper* 'Happy Birthday', Croz. The other one.

Crosby   What other one?

Gilbert   The squashed tomatoes and stew one.

Crosby   I don't know that one, Gilbert.

> *A song-sheet drops in, bearing the words of the song,
> so the audience can sing with the convicts.*

Gilbert   I bet they do. Do you know it, kids? *(Audience: 'Yes!')* Sing
it to Crosby. Are you ready? One, two, three——

Audience   Happy Birthday to you,
Squashed tomatoes and stew,
You look like a monkey,
That comes from the zoo.

Crosby   Oh, terrific! When they sing that to Detective Constable Grummett, he'll go stark, staring, raving round the twist.

Gilbert   And while he's going round the twist, Croz—we're going over
that wall.

Crosby   Do we really have to?

Gilbert   I'm going to find that star before I've finished, Crosby.

Crosby   We haven't even found a ladder yet.

Gilbert   We don't need a ladder. We can climb up on that basket
Come on, Croz—quick! I can hear them sentries coming.

Crosby	Don't forget, kids. 'Advance, fishface, and be fossilized.'
Gilbert	But don't sing 'Happy Birthday' until you're asked, will you?

> *The song-sheet is flown. Gilbert and Crosby go off and, immediately, Mullins and MacBain return, from opposite directions. They take up their positions in front of the sentry-boxes.*

MacBain	'Ello, 'ello, 'ello?
Mullins	'Evening, all!
MacBain	It's a grand life acting a member of the British Army!
Mullins	I'm enjoying every minute.
MacBain	It's a regular piece of cake, marching up and down, no words to learn.
Mullins	Where did you go to?
MacBain	Out through the stage door and right round the block.
Mullins	Same here. I popped into a café for a quick cup of tea and a jam doughnut.
MacBain	I stopped off for a cup of coffee and a cheese roll. I'll tell you what I am looking forward to—when somebody comes along and all these boys and girls shout our lines out for us.
Mullins	I can't wait.
MacBain	You won't have to, Mr Mullins, there's somebody coming now. Don't forget, kids. Halt, who goes whatsit.
Mullins	And then, Advance, friend, and thingemebob.

> *MacBain and Mullins quiver with anticipatory delight. Grummett enters. MacBain pushes his rifle out.*

Audience	Halt, who goes there? Friend or foe?
Grummett	Friend.
Audience	Advance, fishface, and be fossilized!
Grummett	What? What! Say that again?
Audience	Advance, fishface, and be fossilized.
Grummett	Fishface? Fossilized? Charming. *(Turning to MacBain and Mullins)* I suppose that was your idea of a joke?
Mullins & MacBain	No.
Grummett	Don't try and come the abdabs with me! You must have put the audience up to it. You're not telling me that those little horrors thought of it themselves.
MacBain	We didn't.
Mullins	We wouldn't, Detective Constable Grummett.
Grummett	*(to the audience)* Then who did?
Audience	Gilbert and Crosby!
Grummett	Gilbert and Crosby! That's all I need is that. I come to the theatre to see a Chrissie play. I find it overrun with desperate

criminals. And when I try to put the play to rights, what thanks do I get? None. No. I get called 'Fishface' instead. And told to get fossilized. Charming. Can't some of you grown-ups control them kids? *(He blows his nose, loudly, close to tears)* That's very nice, isn't it? That's just the sort of name—Fishface, you like to be called on your birthday.

Mullins   Is it your birthday, Detective Constable Grummett.

> *Grummett nods, blows his nose again, and enjoys a little private grief in a corner as MacBain and Mullins talk in whispers.*

MacBain   Do you think we ought to try and cheer him up?

Mullins   Have you got any ideas?

MacBain   Supposing we sing 'Happy Birthday' to him?

Mullins   By ourselves? That wouldn't be much of a treat.

MacBain   We could get the audience to sing it to him as well.

Mullins   You're right. We could. That would really put him back on his feet.

MacBain   You all know 'Happy Birthday', don't you, kids? *(Audience: 'Yes!')* We're going to sing it as a surprise for Detective Constable Grummett. Will you all join in? *(Audience: 'Yes!')* Wait till I count three. *(He calls across to Grummett who is still sniffling in his handkerchief)* Detective Constable Grummett?

Grummett   What is it?

MacBain   Have you got a moment?

Grummett   What for?

Mullins   It's a surprise, Detective Constable Grummett. A secret.

Grummett   If this is another of your silly tricks, I don't want to know about it.

MacBain   It's not a trick, Detective Constable Grummett. It's a birthday treat. Ready, kids? One, two, three . . .

> *Unseen by Grummett or the Constables, the song-sheet drops in again. Crosby and Gilbert tip-toe on stage and, again unseen, assist the audience with the song.*

Audience   Happy birthday to you,
Squashed tomatoes and stew,
You look like a monkey,
That comes from the zoo!

> *Grummett is incensed. Mullins and MacBain are cross, too, they run up and down, shaking their fists at the audience as Grummett speaks. Behind them, Gilbert and Crosby are making their bid to climb over the wall.*

Grummett   You little monsters! You rotten little horrors! I'll get my own back on you cheeky little ruffians before this play is through!

(To MacBain and Mullins) And you two can say your own words in future, not leave them to be said by a gang of scruffy ragamuffins! *(And, without turning round, he bellows)* And I can see you, too, Gilbert and Crosby, I've got eyes in the back of my head!

> *Gilbert and Crosby freeze on the prop basket as Grummett swings round, producing his gun.*

Orlright. Hold it. The game's up. And get down off that basket. That's *my* basket. You've got no right to touch that basket.

> *Gilbert and Crosby get down.*

Gilbert   We didn't hurt it, Detective Constable Grummett. We only borrowed it to stand on.

Grummett   That's full of very important panto clothes, that basket is. I don't want your dirty hoof-prints all over the lid. Stand over there. Guard them, lads.

> *MacBain and Mullins stand guard over Gilbert and Crosby while Grummett crosses to examine his basket. As he speaks, Grummett opens the lid of the basket, sticks in his hand without looking, and pulls out an enormous hairy spider on a length of elastic.*

Ow! Oooh! Help! Mother! Take it away, I don't like it!

MacBain ⎫
Mullins ⎬ Oooooooerr! Eeeee-ow!
         ⎭

> *And Mullins and MacBain cling to each other for protection.*

Gilbert   Run for it, Croz!

> *Gilbert and Crosby snatch at opportunity and make their escape into the audience. Grummett, holding the spider at arm's length, rounds on MacBain and Mullins.*

Grummett   Get after them, you clod-hopping constables! I want that pair of criminals apprehended and behind bars before this play continues!

> *Mullins and MacBain pursue Gilbert and Crosby through the auditorium. Grummett regains the audience's attention by blowing several short, sharp blasts on his whistle. He continues to hold the jiggling spider, on the end of the elastic, at arm's length.*

Yes, you lot. I wasn't blowing this whistle for my own amusement. You've managed to do it again, haven't you? Call yourselves honest, upright, law-abiding citizens? I should cocoa! I've had more help from audiences in Strangeways Prison than what I've had from you. I suppose you think it's funny, hiding horrible, hairy spiders in theatrical baskets? Well, believe you me, somebody's going to suffer for it before I'm through. I am going off now to get rid of this horrible monstrosity. I shall dispose of it either down the lavvy or at London Zoo. I shall be gone for something like ten minutes. So you lot just behave yourselves, sit up straight, cut out the chatter, face front, and watch your manners while I'm gone. 'Squashed tomatoes and stew'? You impertinent whippersnappers. I'll have the lot of you in Wormwood Scrubs if you don't brighten your ideas up.

He has at last come to terms with the spider.

Horrible, hairy spiders, indeed! It'll take more than a spindly legged plastic spider to put the wind up Detective Constable Grummett, C.I.D. . . . Yeee-ow!

Grummett bellows with fear as the grinning, green skeleton descends again. He belts offstage.

END OF ACT ONE

ACT TWO
Scene One

The stage is exactly as we left it at the end of Act One: the wall is in position and the prop basket is where Grummett abandoned it.

As the house lights fade down, Grummett enters, eating a tub of ice-cream. He stands scowling at the audience and, when he has swallowed his last mouthful of ice-cream, he takes out his whistle and blows three short, sharp blasts.

Grummett   Yes, that does mean you. So pay attention. I've worked out a new system. Whenever I blow three short, sharp blasts—like so—it means that you cheeky blighters have to cut the cackle and sit up straight. If I blow *four* short, sharp blasts, that means that I require the presence pronto of my constables. Like so.

> *Grummett blows four short, sharp blasts on his whistle and Mullins and MacBain scamper on. They are now back in their policemen's uniforms.*

That's better. Very smartly turned out, the pair of you. At least you *look* like constables.

MacBain   Did you want us, Detective Constable Grummett?

Grummett   Not just now.

Mullins   You blew your whistle.

Grummett   Did I? Oh, yes—I was merely giving these dumb-bells out here a practical illustration of what I use my whistle for. Now that you are here, you can take these away with you and stick them in a dustbin somewhere.

> *Grummett hands Mullins and MacBain his empty ice-cream tub and his spoon.*

Mullins   *(under his breath)* What did your last servant die of?

Grummett   Did you speak?

Mullins   Not me, Detective Constable Grummett, I only coughed.

Grummett   Lucky for you. Any insubordination from either of you, and I'll have you both transferred to another theatre, double-quick. So just watch it—or you'll find yourselves cleaning out the kennels at the Sooty and Sweep Show. Now, get off this stage, smartish, and comb the dressing-rooms for them missing convicts. You heard me—hop it!

> *Mullins and MacBain go off, and Grummett turns his attention to the audience.*

Now pay attention, horrors, stop munching crisps and crinkling toffee papers, and I'll tell you what I've got arranged for the second half of the programme.

> *At which point, Clara enters, still carrying her shopping-bag over her arm, and now holding aloft two empty ice-lolly sticks. She is accompanied by Alexander.*

Clara   Stephen Grummett! At last! I've been all over this theatre looking for you—I didn't get so much as a packet of nuts in the interval.

Grummett   Clara, my love, how many times must I tell you not to bother me when I'm on duty? Alexander, do you have to pick your nose in public? Clara, why are you holding lolly-sticks in the air? Where's the lollies?

Clara   Melted, Stephen. All down my arms. I'm extremely sticky around my elbows, and it's all your fault. You're not supposed to be on duty. You told me you were taking a day off.

Grummett   So I am, dearest. Just as soon as I've arrested a couple of arch-villains and turned this disgusting play into an entertainment fit for our little lad to watch.

Clara   How do you mean, Stephen? You aren't going to try to sing 'If I Ruled The World' again, I hope?

Grummett   Certainly not. Well—not without rehearsing it first. Alexander, don't scribble rude words on the scenery—it doesn't belong to us. I'm putting on a proper panto, Clara. With gossamer-winged fairies and a magic wood. You'd like to see them, Alexander, wouldn't you?

Alexander   No. I'd like to see Dracula best. Can we have Dracula, Dad? Where he bites his fangs into somebody's neck, and there's all these horrible screams and this dripping blood? Can we have that, Dad?

Grummett   No! We are not having violence, lad. It's Christmas. Clara, you'd like to see a fairyland grotto, I know.

Clara   I'd like to see a lavvy first. I want to wash the sticky off my hands. I don't suppose you happen to know if there's a toilet anywhere?

Grummett   There's one on that side—but I don't think it's got a wash-basin.

Clara   Oh, dear.

Grummett   And there's one on that side that has got a wash-basin, but I don't think there's any soap.

Clara   Honestly, Stephen, this theatre's a disgrace. I don't know why you couldn't have taken us somewhere a bit more respectable this year, just for once. Alexander, come along with Mummy.

> *Clara marches off, but Alexander hangs back.*

Alexander   Can't we even have a bit of Dracula, Dad? Can't we have just that bit where they hammer that wooden stake through his heart and his blood gushes out? And there's all blood, all over the scenery and the floor! Can't we, Dad?

Grummett No, we can't! It's the season of goodwill. Push off with your mum before I fetch you one with the back of my hand. Go on—scoot!

> *Alexander scoots. Grummett turns to the audience.*

Sorry about that. I'll have a proper panto going before you can say 'Humpty-Dumpty'. Hang about a sec while I have a sort round in my costume basket and see what togs I can rustle up.

> *Grummett delves in the prop basket and unearths a pointed feathered cap and a wide gold belt.*

What have we here? Prince Charming's hat and Prince Charming's belt. That settles it—we're going to do 'The Sleeping Beauty'. And guess who's going to be Prince Charming?

> *Grummett puts on the cap and the belt, consigning his own bowler hat to the prop basket.*

How's that, then? Righto, mums, dads, teachers, dear little kiddiewinks, our story begins a long, long time ago, far, far away, in a golden land where time stands still. And in this land there slept this beautiful princess who had had the extreme misfortune to prick her finger with this wicked witch's bodkin. That's for starters. Now—can we have this stupid wall got rid of? And the lovely Sleeping Beauty wheeled on instead? Come on, then—shift it. I'm not talking to myself.

> *The wall begins to move.*

That's a bit more like it. Ladies and gentlemen, boys and girls, for your especial pleasure, Detective Constable Grummett Productions proudly present: 'The Sleeping Beauty'!

> *The wall is struck.*

Scene Two

> *As the wall and the sentry-boxes are flown, we discover Mullins and MacBain fast asleep in a couple of chairs on an otherwise empty stage.*

Grummett MacBain! Mullins! What's your game? Get off my stage!

> *But the two constables snore louder than ever. Grummett blows his whistle and they wake with a start.*

MacBain 'Ello, 'ello, 'ello?
Mullins 'Evening, all.
MacBain What's all this 'ere?
Grummett Well might you ask! I thought I told you two idle hounds to

hunt down those desperate criminals? Not to get your heads down, while nobody was looking, behind the scenery. Clear off! I'm trying to get a panto going. *(Calling offstage)* Use your loaves, out there. Make it look good. Let's have some fancy lighting and a bit of magic music, please!

> *At Grummett's request, the stage glows with light and 'magic music' fills the air.*

Better. Better. Now you're trying. Now bring the Sleeping Beauty onstage, please.

> *A glittering truck comes into view and glides slowly forward. On the truck is a splendid throne and, fast asleep on the throne, there sleeps a young lady who is wearing an ermine-trimmed cloak and a diamond-studded tiara.*

God bless us all, it is—it's her! The Sleeping Beauty. Stand back. Here comes the leading lady. *(He calls into the wings)* Well done, out there! *(And next he whispers at MacBain and Mullins, fiercely, out of the corner of his mouth)* Have you pair of constables got cloth ears? I told you to push off. Go on, sling your hooks. *(Then, back to the audience)* Going on with the story, then. Thus it was, because of this wicked witch, who was a real right medieval, hard-case villain, and had done a moody over not getting an invite to the princess's posh, slap-up christening, that the whole country was cast into this deep slumber.

> *Over the above, MacBain and Mullins have been peering at the sleeping figure on the throne.*

MacBain   Excuse us interrupting, Detective Constable Grummett——

Grummett   Buzz off. I wont tell you two again.

Mullins   But Detective Constable Grummett——

Grummett   I mean it, Mullins. Scarper—pronto! *(Then, back to the audience)* And so it was decreed by the powers of evil that this unhappy country would thus remain—flat on its back and out for the count—until the arrival of the brave, handsome and gallant Prince Charming many years later—that's me. Use your imaginations, imagine the passing of the years. Now then, our heroine, the Sleeping Beauty, sleeps on, totally unaware that her handsome rescuer is close at hand——

MacBain   That's just it, Detective Constable Grummett, it isn't——

Grummett   If you don't vamoose, MacBain, this instant, I'll duff you up. *(Back to the audience)* As I was saying, the lovely Sleeping Beauty can only be awakened by a tender kiss and a quick chorus of 'If I Ruled the World'. This is the bit I've been looking forward to since we started. The moment when I plant a firm but gentle kiss on the Sleeping Beauty's pretty mouth. I'll have to do it smartish before the wife gets back.

Mullins   *(in an urgent whisper)* It isn't the Sleeping Beauty, Detective Constable Grummett.

          Grummett pauses in the act of planting the fateful kiss.

Grummett   'Course it is. Hop-it. Blow.
Mullins   It isn't, Detective Constable Grummett. It's Miss Camden Town. *

Grummett   *Who ?*
MacBain   Miss Camden Town, Detective Constable Grummett. That's what we've been trying to tell you. It isn't the Sleeping Beauty at all. It's a Beauty *Queen*. Miss Camden Town. Have a look at that sash she's wearing, if you don't believe us. It's got her name on it.

          Grummet throws open the young woman's cloak to reveal the sash that she is wearing. To his horror, he also discovers that she is wearing a swimming costume.

Grummett   Stone the crows ! She's very nearly starkers ! She's only got a swimming-cozzie on !

          He re-arranges the young lady's cloak, hastily, and glowers into the wings.

          Orlright, orlright—who did it ? Own up. I'm not kidding— somebody on this theatre staff will do fifteen years for this little upset, or else I'm handing in my warrant card. *(To the audience)* And I've a very strong suspicion that you lot aren't entirely blameless either ! *(Back to the young woman)* Madam ! Miss ! Wake up at once ! You can't kip here in the almost altogether ! You're on the stage of the Shaw Theatre. We're in the middle of a kiddies' entertainment ! Wake up, young woman ! I am an official of New Scotland Yard and I must warn you that anything you say will be taken off—I mean taken down . . . *(Then, giving up, he turns back to the audience)* It's no good. It's gone too far, has this. Buckingham Palace scenery. Female persons in their nuddies on the stage. I've had my M.B.E. without a shadow of doubt.

          Grummett sits on the edge of the truck in despair, his head in his hands.

MacBain   What are we going to do now, Detective Constable Grummett ?
Grummett   Jack it in. Give up. I don't stand a dog's chance of getting any- thing going here. *(Then, summoning reserves of endeavour, he leaps to his feet)* No, we're not, lads ! We're going to see it out. Regardless. We're going to nab those desperate criminals and also find out who it is who keeps mucking up my panto. Come on !

                              * Or local place.

MacBain   What about Miss Camden Town?

Grummett   Leave her where she is. In the Land of Nod. I can arrest her any time. We've got bigger fish to fry. Follow me, lads!

> *Grummett goes off, trundling his prop basket, and followed by MacBain and Mullins. Gilbert and Crosby enter from the opposite side. Crosby is carrying a short ladder. They do not see Miss Camden Town, nor do they notice that the wall is gone.*

Gilbert   Now's our chance, Croz. Put the ladder up. Over the wall and after that star while there's nobody about.

Crosby   You and that star, Gillo—I'm sick of hearing about that star. There isn't a star. There never was a star. It's a bit of scenery, that's what your star is—like this wall.

> *With which, and without looking, he leans his ladder against the non-existent wall. He realizes that the wall is no longer there when the ladder falls to the ground.*

It's gone!

Gilbert   What's gone?

Crosby   That wall. Those sentry-boxes. They've disappeared.

Gilbert   Don't be ridiculous, Crosby. Walls and sentry-boxes don't just disappear. They don't move scenery until you've finished using it—— Hey, you're right, Croz. It *has* disappeared.

Crosby   Where do you think it's vanished to?

Gilbert   I don't know. But I'm going to find out. *(He approaches the audience)* Do you know where that wall went, kids?

> *The audience point up above Gilbert and Crosby's heads to where the wall was flown.*

Crosby   Up there? That great big brick wall? *(Audience: 'Yes!')* They wouldn't move a great big heavy wall up there! *(The audience insists that this is so. Crosby covers his head with his hands, in fear)* That's dangerous. Come on, Gilbert, we're getting out of this play. That could come crashing right down on us at any minute!

Gilbert   No, it won't, Croz. It's safe. And look—look over there!

> *He points at the sleeping figure on the throne.*

Crosby   Who's that?

Gilbert   I don't know.

Crosby   That's another person I don't remember seeing before in this play.

> *They tiptoe across and gaze at the sleeping figure.*

What's she doing kipping here?

> *Gilbert puts a finger to his lips and 'shushes' Crosby.*

Gilbert   Don't wake her, Croz. Here, she's smashing, isn't she?

Crosby   *(he shrugs)* Not bad.

Gilbert Not bad? She's better than 'not bad', Crozzo. She's a bit of all right.

Crosby   I've seen worse.

Gilbert I'll bet you haven't seen many better, Croz. She's terrific. I'll tell you what, I wouldn't mind winning her hand.

Crosby   You? You've got no chance, mate. You can forget them ideas.

Gilbert Why?

Crosby   Because you're a villain, Gilbert, that's why. You've got no chance at all. You know that—you've been in Chrissie plays before. It's always the hero that gets the good-looking bird.

Gilbert Yeh. *(Then, a sudden thought)* This play hasn't got a hero, has it, though?

Crosby   No. I always *knew* there was something missing.

> *Miss Camden Town, whose name is Mavis Dawkins, stretches and yawns.*

Gilbert She's waking up.

Mavis   Who are you?

Crosby   Gilbert and Crosby. I'm Crosby, he's Gilbert. We're a pair of desperate criminals.

Gilbert We're not really all that desperate though.

Crosby   We're pretty desperate. He once nicked a whole case of baked beans.

Gilbert Don't tell big fibs, Crosby. I didn't nick them, miss. They fell off the back of a lorry.

Crosby   Detective Constable Grummett won't believe that, Gilly, when he catches up with you. Fell off the back of a lorry!

Gilbert They did.

Crosby   It's the oldest one in the book is that. *(To Mavis)* As a matter of interest—who are you?

> *Mavis reels off her identity parrot-fashion, having done so many times before.*

Mavis   My name is Mavis Dawkins and I hold the title Miss Camden Town. I am a natural blonde with naturally curly hair. I am nineteen years old and I work as a junior hair-stylist. My measurements are thirty-six twenty-six thirty-five. My hobbies are meeting people; making all my own clothes; and supporting Brentford Football Club.* My ambitions are to go on from here and win the Miss World contest; become a famous model; travel all over the world; and eventually become a famous film star.

Crosby   What are you doing in this theatre? You won't become a famous film star here.

---

* Or local club.

Mavis	They held a Beauty Competition here yesterday afternoon.
Gilbert	And did you win it and become Miss Camden Town?
Mavis	No, I won the Miss Camden Town title in August of this year. Yesterday's competition was for the title Miss Greater London Council. *(She bursts into tears)* I lost! I came fourth!

> *Mavis sheds floods of tears, and it is some time before she can be pacified.*

Gilbert	Don't cry. Cheer up, eh? I'll bet you were the best one there. I'll bet it was a fiddle, eh, Croz?
Crosby	Definitely bent—it must have been.
Mavis	Do you think so?
Gilbert	Cross my throat. If Crosby and me had been the judges, you'd be Miss Greater London Council now. Right, Croz?
Crosby	Certainly. You could be Miss Wormwood Scrubs if you came to prison with me.
Gilbert	There you are! How come you lost the competition here?

> *Mavis displays her feet. She is wearing plimsolls.*

Mavis	I think it was my feet that let me down. All the other girls had high-heeled shoes—I only had my plimmies with me.
Gilbert	And you lost the competition because of that? That *proves* it was a fiddle. What's wrong with them? They look fantastic plimmies to me. Come on, give us a smile. It isn't the end of the world, you know. You did come fourth. Think of the poor girl who came last. How must she feel?
Mavis	I did come last. There were only four of us in the competition. Miss Muswell Hill; Miss Chalk Farm; Miss Cricklewood; and mm—mm—mm—mmeee . . .

> *Mavis dissolves into tears again.*

Gilbert	Come on, have my hanky. Dry your eyes. Blow your nose. Go on, give it a good blow. It couldn't have been all that important, if only four girls went in for it.
Mavis	Yes, it was. There were all kinds of breathtaking prizes for the fortunate recipient. A fortnight's dream holiday for two in Felixstowe. A year's supply of canned foods donated by a world-famous canned foods manufacturer. A money voucher to be spent on woolly cardigans in a well-known London store. Even the runner-up got a free night out with the companion of her choice, in a candle-lit West End night-spot, inclusive of w—w—w—wine . . .

> *She is in floods of tears again.*

Crosby	Buck up. You can't cry here, miss. You're holding up the Chrissie play.
Gilbert	Why don't you nip off home, eh? And get your head down? You'll feel better in the morning.

Crosby	What are you doing here anyway, if the competition was yesterday?
Mavis	Because I can't go home, can I? Not now. I'll be a laughing-stock. I told them I was going to be a star. And I only came f—f—f—fourth . . .
Gilbert	If you want my opinion, being a star's not all that much to shout about.
Crosby	It isn't, no. The feller who thinks he's the star of this show is a Detective Constable who runs away when he sees a plastic skelegog.
Gilbert	It's true. Crosby and me are looking for a *real* star. Aren't we, Croz?
Crosby	So you keep telling me.
Gilbert	Hey, Crozzie! I've just had a great idea!
Crosby	Oh, no! Not another one.
Gilbert	Why don't we let her come with us.
Crosby	Come with us where?
Gilbert	To look for the star.
Crosby	Do you mean, let her be in the play?
Gilbert	Yes.
Mavis	Can I really? Say that I can—I'll be the happiest girl in all the world.
Crosby	You can't—no.

Mavis's lower lip trembles, dangerously.

Gilbert	Go on, Croz. Don't be rotten.
Crosby	No. Don't you ever learn, Gilly? Haven't we had enough trouble with Detective Constable Grummett poking his nose in? Look at the mess we're in now. Do you know where this plot's going? Because I don't. It's bad enough letting in people from the audience, without having to work with any Tom, Dick or Mavis who happens to be hanging around backstage. No.
Gilbert	Be a sport, Croz.
Mavis	I'll try ever so hard to be a credit to my chosen profession.
Gilbert	She won't get in the way.
Crosby	For the final time, Gilly—N—O: no!

Mavis bursts into tears again.

Gilbert	Now see what you've done.
Crosby	Not that again! All right—go on. I stand for it every time. You can be in the play.

> *Mavis stops crying as quickly as she started, and beams:*

Mavis	What part do I get? What do I have to do?

Crosby	Nothing. Just keep quiet and stick close to us. We'll do all the acting.
Mavis	Can I have my name in lights? Do I get a chauffeur-driven Rolls-Royce? Am I in the number-one dressing-room?
Gilbert	Not to begin with.
Crosby	She's only got a walk-on part, what does she want the number-one dressing-room for?
Mavis	So that I can have it thronged with rich young lords and handsome racing-car drivers, all drinking champagne out of my plimmies.
Crosby	I knew she was going to be trouble.
Mavis	And can I have some words? I'm bursting with talent. Watch. *(She goes into a hammy audition routine)* Cinderella: 'Oh, please, Ugly Sisters—mayn't I go to the ball? Don't leave me here in the kitchen with the rats and mice.' Dick Whittington: 'Twenty more miles to London Town, pussy—and these plimmies are crippling my feet.' Babes in the Wood: 'Don't cry, little brother, let us lie down under this tree and let the kind birdies and bunnikins cover us with——'
Crosby	Shut up! Put a sock in it.
Gilbert	It's not that kind of Chrissie play.
Mavis	What kind is it?
Gilbert	Sort of cops and robbers. Crozzo and me are the robbers——

> *At which point, MacBain and Mullins enter, blowing their whistles.*

Here come the cops. Run for it!

> *Macbain and Mullins pursue Gilbert, Crosby and Mavis through the audience. As the two criminals and the beauty queen make their escape, Grummett enters, again pushing the prop basket.*

Grummett	Settle down, nuisances, let's have a bit of hush. I've had another go at getting things sorted out—I think I've managed it. Arrests are pending. Also, and appertaining to the panto, I've found a wardrobe lady round the back who's got a room that's crammed to the door with panto clothes. All washed and ironed. *(He waves a deprecating hand at the prop basket)* It's ten times better than this old rubbish. So what we're going to do is——

> *He breaks off as Mullins and MacBain return, out of breath and flustered.*

Where've you two idle so-and-so's been?

MacBain	Chasing them desperate criminals round and round the audience, like you told us.
Mullins	Miss Camden Town's gone with them.

Grummett   That comes as no surprise to me. I've cracked this case at last.
           I reckon it's her that's been messing about with my scenery.

MacBain   Miss Camden Town? What for?

Grummett   Because she's not who she says she is. Did you ever see a
           Beauty Queen before in plimmies?

           MacBain and Mullins shake their heads.

           They always wear high-heels. She's an actress, that's who she
           is—purporting to be a Beauty Queen. You're not observant,
           are you? That's why I'm with the C.I.D. while you two are only
           enacting the roles of uniformed police.

Mullins   Can't we be something else? I'm fed up with always playing
           constable parts.

MacBain   Me too. It's not what I call proper acting, chasing people
           through the audience.

Grummett   You're neither of you acting anything until you've done your
           duty. I want three arrests made—two criminals pretending to be
           actors, and one actress pretending to be a Beauty Queen. Get
           on with it.

Mullins   Do we have to?

MacBain   Give us a break, Detective Constable Grummett. Be a sport.
           Can't we be the panto horse?

Grummett   No. But you're going to get your chance to be something
           different. We're not doing the 'Sleeping Beauty' any longer.
           We're doing another panto and there's two parts in it for you.

MacBain   What's the panto?

Mullins   What are we going to be?

Grummett   'Aladdin and his Wonderful Lamp. You can be Wishee and
           Washee—a couple of crazy Chinese constables.

MacBain   Policemen's parts again.

Mullins   I might have known it.

Grummett   I shall essay the role of Abanazar, the wicked magician. I've
           got a smashing costume in the wardrobe room. Once I've got
           it on, I might treat the audience to a quick chorus of 'If I Ruled the
           World', while I'm waiting for you. Go get about your duties, lads
           —real life comes first. We're not beginning anything until Gilbert,
           Crosby and that phantom female scenery-shifter are safely in the
           nick. Move!

           *MacBain and Mullins go off. Grummett addresses the
           audience, declaiming with grandiose gestures:*

           Each Christmastime
           King Pantomime doth rule,
           And at his bidding
           Let these lights go down,
           That in the darkness
           May the scene be set—

A bright and sunny day
In Peking's Chinatown!

The lights fade.

Scene Three

Total darkness on the stage. Gilbert, Crosby and Mavis enter from the back of the auditorium.

Gilbert	Come on, Croz. Don't dawdle. Not far now.
Mavis	Where are we going?
Gilbert	Back on the stage. To follow that star.
Mavis	What star?
Crosby	There isn't a star. He's got stars on the brain. He imagines stars.

A pinpoint of light shines in the darkness on the stage.

Gilbert	All right, clever-clogs. What's that there?
Mavis	There *is* a star! I can see it, too! Do you think it's the star on my dressing-room door?
Crosby	It's definitely not a Chrissie star. It never is. It always turns out to be something else.
Gilbert	Stop moaning, Crosby. I'll bet it is the Chrissie star this time.

They move up on to the darkened stage. The lights come up, slowly, and they find themselves in a large, gloomy room full of mysterious shadowy corners and creepy arched windows. There is a heavy, iron-studded door. The 'star' turns out to be the light of a tall candle, set in the wall at the back of the room. The prop basket is still set, centre-stage, where Grummett left it.

Crosby	What did I say? You've only been and gone and done it again, Gilly. Star! Trust you. Who else would mistake a candle for a star?
Mavis	Where are we supposed to be?
Gilbert	Don't ask me. I've never seen this scenery before.
Crosby	I hope I never have to see it again. It's a bit too creepy for a Chrissie play, is this place, if you ask me.
Mavis	It reminds me of something—but I can't think what.
Gilbert	It doesn't remind me of anything to do with the play we're supposed to be doing.
Mavis	Hey! I know what it is—where it reminds me of. It's suddenly come to me. Do you know where it looks exactly like?
Crosby	Where?

Mavis	Have you ever seen any Dracula films?
Crosby	*(terrified)* Count Dracula? He's not about, is he?
Gilbert	*(to Mavis)* Don't frighten him. He doesn't like it.
Mavis	It does. This scenery looks just like Dracula's house.
Crosby	Oh, Gilbert! I hate Dracula. I do, I really hate him. He scares the wits out of me. Can't we stop being in this play now?
Gilbert	Don't pay any attention to her, Croz. This isn't supposed to be Dracula's house.
Crosby	Are you sure?
Gilbert	'Course I am.
Crosby	How can you tell?
Gilbert	Because if it was there'd be a big, black coffin in the middle of the room. He sleeps in a coffin, does Dracula, and he only comes out at the dead of night.

> *Mavis glances around the room and takes in the moonlight streaming in at the window.*

Mavis	I think it's supposed to be dead of night now.
Crosby	I'm getting out of here. *(He rushes across to the iron-studded door, but finds it locked)* It's bolted from the outside. We're locked in Dracula's room at the dead of night. Save us, somebody! Help us! Let us out!
Gilbert	Calm down, Croz. I've told you—there'd be a coffin in here if it was Dracula's house. Can you see anything that looks like a coffin?

> *Crosby's eyes scan the room anxiously, and he gazes at the prop basket.*

Crosby	How about that?
Gilbert	That's Detective Constable Grummett's prop basket. That's full of old theatrical costumes.
Crosby	But supposing Dracula's crept into it?
Gilbert	Don't be ridiculous, Crosby.
Crosby	He might have done.
Gilbert	What for?
Crosby	For his daytime kip. To keep the sun out of his eyes. Supposing they didn't have a coffin for him in the prop room? Supposing they've had to use Grummett's basket instead?
Gilbert	That's stupid.
Crosby	Yes—but have a look in it for me, just to make sure. Go on, Gilly. Be a pal.
Gilbert	Look inside yourself.
Crosby	I daredn't.
Gilbert	I'm not looking for you.
Mavis	If he is in there, Count Dracula——
Gilbert	He isn't in there.

Mavis   But if he is, do you know what happens? The lid opens ever so slowly, and a sinister, creepy hand reaches out and feels along the edge.

Crosby   Oh, Gilly! What if he is!

Mavis   And he comes to life. And he sits up in his coffin. And he has these red-rimmed eyes and these horrible fangs. It isn't half scary. It's ever so good.

Crosby rushes to the door again and hammers on it.

Crosby   Let me out! Let me out! There's Dracula in here in a clothes basket!

Gilbert   He isn't, Crosby. Pull yourself together. *(To Mavis)* I do wish you'd stop putting the wind up him. It's bad enough being locked in here. Perhaps there's a secret passage somewhere. All start looking round the walls.

Crosby   You've got to be joking, Gilbert? What if the sinister, creepy hand opens up that lid while we're searching over there?

Gilbert   There isn't a sinister, creepy hand.

Crosby   But supposing there is!

Gilbert   If it will make you feel any better, Croz, we'll ask the audience to keep an eye on the basket for us.

Crosby   That'd be great. Do you think they will?

Gilbert   We can but try. Will you, kids? And give us a shout if you see anything coming out of that basket? *I* know there's nothing in there—but it'll stop Crosby getting the jim-jams. So will you do it for us? *(Audience: 'Yes!')* There you are.

Crosby   Thanks, kids.

Gilbert   Now help me look for a secret passage.

Gilbert, Crosby and Mavis search the walls for a secret passage. While they are doing so, the lid of the prop basket opens, slowly, and a sinister, creepy hand feels its way along the edge of the basket. Pandemonium from the audience. The hand slips back into the basket and the lid closes.

(To the audience) What is it? What's the matter?

Gilbert, Crosby and Mavis ad-lib a conversation with the screaming audience, during which they restore some sort of order and also ascertain what it is that has caused the screaming. Then:

Gilbert   A what, kids? A hand came out of that basket?

Audience   Yes!

Crosby   Oooh, Gilly!

Mavis   Was it all sinister and creepy?

Audience   Yes!

Crosby   I knew that Dracula was in that basket. I told you so.

Gilbert   He isn't in there. They're having you on, Crosby. *(Audience: 'No, we're not!')* Yes, you are! There wasn't a hand. *(Audience: 'Yes, there was!')* I don't believe you.

Crosby   I believe them, Gilbert.

Mavis   I believe them, too.

Gilbert   Well, I don't. I don't believe that Dracula would go to sleep in a prop basket. He has his posh coffin, and that's the only place he gets his head down.

> *But while Gilbert has been speaking, the sinister, creepy hand has appeared again. Gilbert's words are drowned as the audience goes wild. This time, Gilbert, Crosby and Mavis also catch a glimpse of the sinister hand before it slips back into the basket again. In the general pandemonium, Mavis suffers near-hysterics. Gilbert, ad-libbing, has to calm down all three: Crosby, Mavis and the audience. And, when order is once more restored:*

          Is everybody calm again? Because I'll tell you what we're going to do.

Crosby   I know what I'm going to do, Gilbert—the four-minute mile, if I can break down that door.

Gilbert   Shut up, Croz. And listen to me. If Dracula comes out of that basket, we're going to frighten him away.

Crosby   We're—going—to—what?

Gilbert   Scare him.

Crosby   Scare Dracula?

Gilbert   That's right.

Crosby   By ourselves? Us three? Alone?

Gilbert   But we're not alone, are we? We've got all these kids to help us.

Crosby   They won't help us. They're as scared as we are.

Mavis   Yes, they will. Won't you, kids? *(Audience: 'Yes!')* There you are.

Gilbert   Now there are lots of us.

Crosby   You still haven't told me *how* we're going to frighten Dracula?

Gilbert   We're going to work out what it is he's scared of. Everybody's scared of something. So if we can find out what it is that puts the wind up vampires, we'll be all right.

Mavis   I know something! Big wooden stakes with sharp points. That's how you kill Dracula—you plunge a wooden stake into his heart.

Gilbert   That's not a bad idea. Hands up all the kids who've brought with them a big wooden stake with a sharp end?

Crosby   There's a kid up there has got a pencil with a broken point.

Gilbert   That's no good. We'll have to think of something else.

Crosby	Hey, Gilly ! What about the spooky green, grinning skelegog ?
Mavis	What's that ?
Gilbert	It's a plastic skeleton. We keep it up there. We could use that, yes, but it won't be enough on its own.
Mavis	What about a mirror ?
Gilbert	What do we want a mirror for ?
Mavis	Because they don't like mirrors, vampires. Vampires haven't got reflections, so they don't like looking in mirrors.
Gilbert	We haven't got a mirror though.

Mavis produces a pocket mirror.

Mavis	I've got this little one. I always carry it about with me for Beauty Competitions.
Gilbert	Right then, that's the mirror and the skelegog.

Crosby jumps up and down with excitement.

Crosby	I've got it ! I've got it ! I've got it ! I've remembered what else Dracula can't stand.
Gilbert	What's that ?
Crosby	The sign of the cross.
Mavis	He's right. He hates crosses, does Dracula.
Crosby	Except we haven't got a cross, have we ?
Gilbert	We can make them. We can make lots and lots of them. With a bit of help from the audience. Stand up, kids. *(The audience gets to its feet)* Now do this. *(Gilbert stands up straight and extends his arms. The audience does the same)* How's that for crosses ?
Crosby	That's fantastic !
Mavis	That'll really spook Dracula.
Gilbert	Thanks, kids. Great. Sit down. Now, we've got three things : the skelegog ; the sign of the cross ; and Mavis's mirror. What we need now is a signal. When I drop my hand—like this—can you all shout, 'Wheeeee !' ? *(Audience: 'Yes!')* Let's hear you. *(The audience shouts: 'Wheeeee!')* And now let me hear you do a 'Whooooo !' *(The audience goes 'Whooooo!')* That's fine. Now, this is what we're going to do. When Dracula gets out of his basket, and I drop my hand, you all go 'Wheeeee !' And that'll be the signal for the skelegog to drop. Then, when Crosby drops his hand, you all jump to your feet, make the sign of the cross and go 'Whooooo !' And one other thing—can you all shout 'Hop it, Dracula !' ? Let's hear you. *(The audience shouts: 'Hop it, Dracula!')* Not bad. Because when Mavis sticks her mirror up to Dracula's face, and he can't see his own reflection, that's what I want you all to shout : 'Hop it, Dracula !' Have you got it now ? My hand, 'Wheeeee !' And the skelegog. Crosby's hand, 'Whooooo !' and the sign of the cross. Mavis's mirror, 'Hop it, Dracula !' Shall we have a rehearsal ? I'll be

Dracula. Crozzo, you drop your hand for me. Ready? This is Dracula coming out of his coffin.

> *Gilbert lumbers forward, menacingly. Crosby drops his hand. The audience goes 'Wheeeeel' and the skeleton dangles in front of Gilbert. Gilbert staggers away, towards the audience. Crosby drops his hand again. The audience leaps to its feet, makes the sign of the cross and goes 'Whooooo!' Gilbert staggers back again. Mavis holds up the mirror in Gilbert's face. Crosby again drops his hand. The audience shouts 'Hop it, Dracula!' Gilbert simulates fear, then:*

That's exactly right, kids. He'll jump straight back in his coffin if we do all that. Now, all we've got to wait for——

> *But Gilbert's words are drowned by the shrieks of the audience as the basket lid opens again, slowly. The sinister hand creeps along the edge of the basket once again. Gilbert 'shushes' the more exuberant members of the audience:*

Quiet, kids. Don't forget, 'Wheeeee!' first, then 'Whooooo!' and the sign of the cross, and 'Hop it, Dracula!' when Mavis shows him the mirror—but wait for the hand signals, won't you?

> *Gilbert, Crosby and Mavis take up their hiding-places. The basket lid opens with agonizing slowness. A terrifying figure stands up in the basket. It has huge fangs; red-rimmed eyes; is wearing full evening dress and has a gold medallion round its neck. The figure's black hair is combed straight back. In short, it would indeed appear that Dracula has risen from his tomb. The Dracula figure clambers out of the basket. Gilbert drops his hand. The audience screams 'Wheeeeel' The grinning, green skeleton drops down and dangles in front of the Dracula figure. The Dracula figure turns away and lumbers towards the audience. Crosby gives the second signal, the audience goes 'Whooooo!' as it leaps to its feet and makes the sign of the cross. Again the figure turns and staggers away. Mavis holds up her mirror as the Dracula figure approaches her. Gilbert again gives the signal and the audience yells out 'Hop it, Dracula!' But, to everybody's surprise, the Dracula figure takes the mirror out of Mavis's hand and, looking into it, doffs his wig and takes out his fangs.*

Dracula   *(he silences the screaming audience first)* Quiet! Can we have a little hush, please! *(He hands the mirror back to Mavis)* Many thanks. I couldn't speak when I had those fangs in.

Gilbert	Aren't they real, then?
Dracula	Of course they're not real. Who do you take me for?
Crosby	Aren't you Dracula?
Dracula	Do I look like Dracula?

> *At which point, Grummett bursts into the room through the iron-studded door. He is wearing his Abanazar costume and brandishing his revolver.*

Grummett	All right, I've got the lot of you red-handed. Come on! Hands up. I've been hiding behind that door, holding it shut, waiting for the opportune moment. This is it. Gilbert and Crosby, you two first, get over there.

> *Gilbert and Crosby raise their hands and back away.*

Grummett	And you, self-styled Miss Camden Town, or whatever other alias you choose to call yourself.
Mavis	But I am Miss Camden Town.
Grummett	A likely story. The phantom scenery shifter, that's who you are. Move!

> *Mavis raises her hands and joins Gilbert and Crosby.*

You as well, Dracula. Join your partners in crime.

Dracula	Are you addressing me?
Grummett	I'm not talking to myself. I'm nicking you for appearing in spooky plays in the festive season.
Dracula	Do you know who you are talking to?
Grummett	No, but I know what I'm talking to—a rotten actor, matey. I've got your number.

> *With a flourish, Dracula removes the black wig that he is wearing and announces his true identity.*

Mayor	I'll have you know, sir, that I happen to be the Mayor of Camden Town. *
Gilbert Mavis Crosby }	The Mayor of Camden Town?
Grummett	Yes, and I'm his Highness, Dick Whittington—I don't think. Pull the other one, it's got bells on.
Mayor	I tell you, man, I am the Mayor.
Grummett	Then perhaps you can explain what you're doing on this stage?
Mayor	Certainly. I was looking into that prop basket in the wings when some clumsy buffoon slammed the lid down on me and wheeled me on.
Grummett	And I suppose you've also got a reason why you were wearing that wig and why you had them fangs in your gob?

* Or local place.

Mayor	Of course. They were in the prop basket and, naturally, in the dark I tried them on. Wouldn't you?
Grummett	And what about your red-rimmed eyes? Why have you got them?
Mayor	Perfectly simple—because I've been up all night, looking for her.
Mavis	Me?
Mayor	If you are Miss Camden Town.
Mavis	Of course I am.
Mayor	Thank heaven for that. I'll come to you later. *(Back to Grummett)* Of course I'm the Mayor, you nincompoop! *(Holding out his medallion)* What do you think this is?
Grummett	A piece of painted cardboard that you got from the wardrobe lady—— Hang on a tick, it's real.
Mayor	Of course it's real—and so am I. Now, perhaps, you'll be good enough to tell me who you are?
Grummett	Detective Constable Grummett, sir. New Scotland Yard.
Mayor	A detective constable—in that ridiculous get-up?

Grummett looks at his Abanazar costume.

Grummett	Ah! There's a very good reason for this costume, sir.
Mayor	There'd better be.
Grummett	You don't have to take my word, sir. Ask my two constables, they'll testify on my behalf. They're a couple of highly responsible actors who've been playing policemen's parts for years.

Grummett blows several short, sharp blasts on his whistle. A pantomime horse enters, gallops round the stage and bows to Grummett, who is not amused.

	You pair of blithering idiots! I said you couldn't be the panto horse.
Mayor	A New Scotland Yard detective dressed as Abanazar? His uniformed constables appearing as a panto horse? I shall be reporting this to your superior officers, Grummett.
Grummett	There's a perfectly logical reason for everything. I was after these two felons, for a kick-off. I was also trying to organize a proper panto, only somebody's been messing up my scenery—all my suspicions fall on her.
Mayor	As far as the entertainment was concerned, Grummett, these two chaps were getting on famously until you stuck your hooter in. And they've my permission to shoot off now and get on with it.
Grummett	Shoot off? They're wanted on a dozen different charges. They escaped from this very theatre in a Christmas play last year.
Mayor	And they're free to do the same again. This audience came here

today to see an entertainment. Go on, Gilbert and Crosby, get yourselves ready for the final scene.

Gilbert   Thanks, Mr Mayor. I promise you I won't give you cause to regret your decision.

Crosby   Same here, sir. I'll really act my best in the scene that's coming next. No hard feelings, Detective Constable Grummett—I hope you enjoy your turkey and custard.

Grummett   I'll get you yet, Gilbert and Crosby. Same time, same place, next year.

Gilbert   Merry Christmas, Detective Constable Grummett.

> *Gilbert and Crosby go off. The Mayor turns back to Grummett.*

Mayor   Now, Grummett, as far as messing up the scenery goes—I caught a glimpse of who was doing that through a peep-hole in that wicker basket.

> *The Mayor crosses to a side wall and calls into a shadowy corner.*

Come on! Out of there. You've caused enough damage for one performance.

> *A figure steps out of the wings—it is Alexander Grummett.*

There's your phantom scenery shifter, Grummett.

Grummett   Alexander? My own son? I don't believe it. You haven't, have you, Alex? Tell me you haven't been touching them ropes and switches that alter the scenery about?

Alexander   Only a few of them, Dad.

Grummett   You little blighter! You mischievous beggar. You're worse than the cheeky horrors in the audience. Come here. Come over here at once, and I'll give you a Chrissie prezzie round your ear-hole.

> *Clara Grummett enters.*

Clara   You lay so much as a finger on my precious baby's head, Stephen Grummett, and there'll be no Chrissie pud for you tomorrow. No, and not so much as a sniff of a mince-pie neither!

Grummett   Do you know what he's guilty of, Clara?

Clara   I know what you're guilty of—coming up here and ruining the play.

Grummett   I was only trying to make it a little more palatable, dear.

Clara   You've made it totally indigestible. *And* covered my arms in sticky—there's not a serviceable lavvy with a wash-basin in this theatre anywhere. I'm only thankful that this gentleman put a stop to things before you got started on 'If I Ruled the World'.

Mayor   She's right, you know. I think that this performance should be a lesson for us all. It shows what trouble can be caused when members of the audience get mixed up with what's happening on the stage. I think it's time you left the theatre now—the stage door's this way.

Grummett   But I've bought and paid for three seats in the stalls!

Mayor   You should have thought of that when you left them. And you can show this panto horse to its dressing-room on the way. *(To the panto horse)* And you should stick to constable parts in future.

A voice emanates from the head of the panto horse.

MacBain   'Ello, 'ello, 'ello? 'Evening, all! What's all this 'ere?

Grummett   That's enough from you. Come on, my lot. Better luck next year.

Grummett leads off the Panto Horse, Clara and Alexander. The Mayor turns to Mavis.

Mayor   And now, before we let Gilbert and Crosby get on with their play, it only remains for me to announce the first piece of good news for the day.

Mavis   Is it to do with me?

Mayor   You look like being the new Miss Greater London Council. *

Mavis   But I only came fourth in the competition.

Mayor   We've since discovered that the winner, Miss Muswell Hill, is married. She's been disqualified.

Mavis   What about Miss Chalk Farm? *

Mayor   We found out she was wearing a wig. It's against the rules.

Mavis   There's still Miss Cricklewood. *

Mayor   Her boyfriend made a fuss about her appearing in public in a swimming-cozzie—she's withdrawn.

Mavis   Is it really me? *(Then, suddenly downcast)* But I can't be Miss Greater London Council. I've only got these old plimmies.

Mayor   Not if I've got anything to do with it. That's what I was looking for in that basket. *(He crosses, opens the basket, and takes out a pair of glass slippers)* These. They used them in a panto here a couple of years ago. If these slippers fit, the first prize is yours.

Mavis   *(examining them)* They're just my size!

Mayor   Congratulations, Miss G.L.C.!

Mavis bursts into tears.

What's the matter?

Mavis   Nothing. It's just that I'm so h—h—h—happy.

The Mayor puts a comforting arm around Mavis's shoulders, and leads her away as the lights fade.

* Or local name.

Scene Four

Gilbert and Crosby enter from the back of the audi-torium.

Crosby   Do we *have* to, Gilbert?

Gilbert   I do wish you'd stop moaning, Crosby.

Crosby   But why do we have to come on again? That seemed like a perfectly good ending to me.

Gilbert   Because we have to find the star.

Crosby   You and that star!

Gilbert   There will be a star, Croz. A real Chrissie star, too, twinkling away.

Crosby   To be quite honest, I don't really care. I don't care if there's a whole galaxy. I hate stars. I do, Gilly, I really hate them. As a matter of fact, I'm not all that struck on moons, either.

Gilbert   Look, Crosby! Down there!

Crosby   Hey! There is a star!

It is true. This time there is no doubt. A star hangs centre-stage, caught in a narrow beam of light.

Gilbert   What did I tell you? Come on! It's getting brighter, Crozzo—all the time!

The lights come up. We are back in Gilbert and Crosby's attic. The star turns out to be a cardboard and silver paper one on top of a Christmas tree. The attic has been gaily decorated with seasonal trimmings, and there is a large, gift-wrapped package.

Crosby   It's not a real star at all. It's only one on a Chrissie tree.

Gilbert   But it's *our* tree, Croz. It's in our attic. The stage manager must have put all these trimmings up. Doesn't it look pretty?

Crosby   *(unimpressed)* Great. That's all I need. All this running around, keeping these kids amused, and we finish up back where we started.

They are back in the attic room.

Gilbert   Perhaps it's symbolic, Crosby. Perhaps this play's got a message. Do you think it means that where ere you wander, there's no place like home sweet home?

Crosby   No, I think it means that the scenery designer ran out of money. We're having to use the same room twice.

Gilbert   Cheer up, Crozzie. Look at this Chrissie prezzie. There's a note with it. *(He opens the note)* It's from Mavis. 'Dear Gilbert and Crosby. Just a line to let you know that I am using up my first prize and having a dream winter holiday for two in Felixstowe.

	The Mayor of Camden Town kindly consented to come with me. He is a nice, thoughtful man, and he has promised to help me become Miss World. Felixstowe is so beautiful. I haven't stopped crying since I got here.'
Crosby	I can believe that, Gilly.
Gilbert	'Your dear friend, Miss G.L.C. P.S.: I am sending you a Chrissie prezzie which was one of my prizes that is no use to me.'

Crosby rips off the wrapping paper.

Crosby	It's a crate of baked beans.

They gaze at each other, horrified, then, seeing the funny side of things, they both begin to laugh.

	Happy Christmas, Gillo.
Gilbert	Happy Christmas, Crozzie—and very many of 'em!
Together	Happy Christmas, kids! Take care of yourselves! See you all again next year!

CURTAIN